The Shoebox Chronicles

By

Mark Gregory Lehman

The Shoebox Chronicles

Trilogy Christian Publishers A Wholly Owned Subsidiary of Trinity Broadcasting Network

2442 Michelle Drive Tustin, CA 92780

Cover design by: Grant Swank

For information about special discounts for bulk purchases, please contact Trilogy Christian Publishing.

Trilogy Disclaimer: The views and content expressed in this book are those of the author and may not necessarily reflect the views and doctrine of Trilogy Christian Publishing or the Trinity Broadcasting Network.

Manufactured in the United States of America

10 9 8 7 6 5 4 3 2 1

Library of Congress Cataloging-in-Publication Data is available.

ISBN: 978-1-63769-422-0

E-ISBN: 978-1-63769-423-7

# Dedication

To my former colleague and friend:

Ruth Lyons

Ruth was the first person to write a comment on my *Shoebox Chronicles* blog page. I have kept her comment on my desk ever since she wrote it, and it reads, "These stories are amazing and really well written. You need to put them in a book."

Thank you, Ruth, for your friendship and your encouragement.

# Table of Contents

Connecting the Dots of Our Lives

"You cannot connect the dots looking forward; you can only connect them looking backwards. So, you have to trust the dots will somehow connect in your future."

Steve Jobs

# Prologue

Recently, I began the laborious and sentimental task of dismantling my parents' homestead. As I perused through old dusty boxes, found tucked away in closets and under beds, I made numerous unique discoveries about my family's journey to the twenty-first century. Most of these discoveries were contained in several shoeboxes stuffed with letters dating back to 1887.

These letters painted a vivid and first-hand account of my family heritage. Through these writings, I began to see my legacy and responsibility in this long line of one family's journey. One letter, dated April 1919 and written in German, articulated how an entire village celebrated the news that my grandaunt and granduncle had purchased property in Texas. The writer, which I believe to be my great-grandaunt, was ecstatic when she wrote, "None of us could have ever believed a member of our family would ever get to own property again. While I miss you terribly, you made the right decision to immigrate to America."

I also learned about two descendants killed while fighting oppression and tyranny in World War II. I discovered how my entire family, both in America and in Germany, provided lifesaving aid to Jewish relatives hiding in Switzerland from Nazis during the Holocaust.

I read with pride about how our family ultimately rallied to support our first interracial marriage in 1951 and how this action led to a lifelong family dedication to civil rights. I discovered a family member who fled to Canada to avoid the draft during the Vietnam Era and that my grandfather proudly purchased the very first Edsel automobile sold in San Antonio, Texas.

To get a better historical perspective of my family history, I spent an entire night organizing the letters by date. Around sunrise, I began to see a disturbing trend emerging. The last letters were dated 1999 as America was in the midst of celebrating one hundred years of what was dubbed "the American Century." We have enjoyed a rich history since that millennial celebration; however, none of our family events are chronicled.

Modern technology has dealt a devastating blow to the art of letter writing. Insignificant Facebook posts, two hundred eighty-character tweets, and easily deleted e-mails have compromised this art. As a result, we could lose very important generational history, which has made the American family the cornerstone of our democracy.

Look no further than the Holy Bible to see the historical impact of the written letters. Almost a third of the New Testament is a compilation of letters written by the apostle Paul to fledgling new churches in places like Corinth,

Thessalonica, and Ephesus. Is there no doubt the New Testament would have been much shorter and less impactful if the apostle Paul would have simply tweeted his messages to the likes of Timothy, Luke, James, and John?

Social communication networks are not going away, and all of us enjoy using these venues to keep up with friends and family, send invitations to happy hours, and forward trivial jokes. However, preserving our history requires a much stronger commitment to the written word. None of us should overlook the generational responsibility of writing and sharing our own histories in diaries, journals, and those all-important letters. These preserved written words are the foundations of any great society, religious movement, or family history.

"Very few of us intentionally connect the truth of the past with the realities of where we have ended up today."

Andy Andrews,
American Author and Speaker

# Living Our History

As I was growing up, it never occurred to me I was creating my own history. I was simply part of the ideal post-war era of the late '50s and early '60s, with loving parents seeking their own part of the American Dream in a brand-new tree-filled subdivision in the hills west of Austin. Our personal safety, exposure to drugs or alcohol, or the infiltration of any non-G-rated programing into our lives was never an issue. Any disruption into my almost idyllic life usually centered around an occasional bee sting, flat tire on my bicycle, or questionable report card from school.

During my formative years, I never thought of my parents as having any type of relationship, romantic or otherwise, outside of tending to the needs of their young family. They were fun-loving and very happy people who seemed content spending their days in a simple routine of putting food on the table, keeping the lawn mowed, and getting their well-groomed children to school and church on time. (Well, most of the time, anyway.)

On occasions like Valentine's Day or their birthdays, they exchanged practical and boring gifts like vacuum cleaners, harvest gold blenders, electric drills, and socks. However, I was enlightened by two letters I recently discovered in the shoebox dated February 1952.

My parents were separated for a few months after their marriage while my dad finished his military obligation. During this time, he wrote a heartfelt letter to his "darling angle" [sic] pledging they would never be separated again. This beautiful, almost poetic letter talked about the home he wanted to build, the children he wanted to have, and the dreams they would share together. He apologized for not being with her on their first Valentine's Day as a married couple and for the fact that she had to settle for a letter instead of her favorite: red roses.

The letter must have made some impact on my mom because she saved it forever. My father also saved the letter she wrote back to him, saying his "sweet words" were all she would ever want from him, and she would be mad if he ever wasted his hard-earned money on something as frivolous as roses.

This simple exchange of words impacted me. They allowed me a unique glimpse into seeing my parents beyond just as providers. They were a young couple in love, planning their lives together. My parents grew up during the Great Depression, where the basics of life were not a certainty. Often, they were not sure where their next meal would come from. The depression years were followed by World War II, where the certainty of the nation was questioned.

These old letters, born from the insecurities of uncertain times, showed my parents had specific childhood dreams of a better life for their own families. During my formative years, my parents watched as their dreams materialized before their very eyes. I now see why they were always so gloriously happy celebrating mundane events like watching *I Love Lucy* on our twelve-inch black and white television, swimming lessons at the public pool, Cub Scouts, and an occasional adventure to the beach.

I now have a clearer understanding of the peace I witnessed the day my dad died. He passed away rather unexpectedly at home just weeks before my parent's fiftieth wedding anniversary. I arrived at their home shortly after receiving the bad news, and I did not know what to expect as I paused at the backdoor before entering. I knew going home would never be the same again. As a child, I always announced my arrival with a boisterous, "Hi everyone! I'm home." I continued the tradition all my life, but it would not be appropriate on this day. I found my mom sitting in her favorite kitchen chair, looking out over their beloved backyard. She looked composed as she mused, "I am so glad we never sold this old house. Your dad's prayer was that God would let him die in the place where all his dreams came true. Today his prayer was answered. God is good."

All of this is a reminder that flowers wilt, pre-printed messages on cards are quickly forgotten, and even toasters and blenders don't come with a lifetime warranty. Written words, saved and passed down through generations, are our only links to our own family histories, legacies, and dreams for future generations to build upon.

My mother often commented on a Bible verse about Jesus' mother realizing her young Son had very special gifts, and Luke 2:51 (NLT) tells us, "Then he returned to Nazareth with them and was obedient to them. And his mother stored all these things in her heart."

By saving these letters and leaving them behind where I would easily find them, my mom left a guidepost about the dreams she was storing in her own heart as a young woman. These dreams later became my reality and my history.

### Preserving the Written Word/ Preserving your History

Had my parents just sent each other sappy pre-printed cards on their first Valentine's Day together, I doubt their messages would have survived all these decades. Card companies make it so easy to find the perfect mass-produced message for any occasion, and all the sender must do is sign their name. By taking the time to hand write sincere personal thoughts on Mother's and Father's Day, birthdays, and Valentine's Day, the card has a greater likelihood of surviving past the next trash pickup day. Who knows, they may even survive long enough to inspire future generations.

# Connecting Generations Through an Unforgotten Grave

> Now, most people would not be willing to die for an upright person, though someone might perhaps be willing to die for a person who is especially good. But God showed his great love for us by sending Christ to die for us while we were still sinners.
>
> Romans 5:7-8 (NLT)

At the end of a long dusty road six miles west of Smiley, Texas (population five hundred and forty-nine), sits a deserted cemetery. It is all that remains of the once-bustling South Texas farming community of Mound Creek.

This is the final resting place for many of my ancestors. I made numerous trips here in my youth to attend funerals. In recent years, occasionally, I would stop by the cemetery when traveling in the area to attend an annual Easter gathering of relatives. I started these visits to Mound Creek to pay respect to some descendants; however, lately, I just enjoy the peace this site provides from urban pressures and chaotic world headlines.

Most of these long-forgotten graves have not seen any attention in decades. The noticeable exception is one single grave located in the far corner of the cemetery next to a barbed-wire fence. This grave stands out among the drab headstones because it is adorned with a colorful Easter bouquet of fresh flowers. During one Easter Sunday visit, curiosity got the best of me, and I looked at the florist's card, which simply read "To Aunt Emily—Love, Johnathan and James."

Immediately this card reminded me of a postcard in the shoebox that I nearly discarded as irrelevant. The undated note was to my grandmother from someone in California named Kate, and the message was, "Johnathan and James are going to a medical conference in San Antonio next month and would like to visit Aunt Em's grave. I cannot find it on the map and hope you can help out."

As I often do with shoebox letters, I use these treasures to connect the dots of family history. My internet searches ultimately led to a distant cousin named Johnathan, who told me a remarkable story about his Aunt Emily, whom he had never met.

Johnathan's grandmother, Kate, was widowed at an early age. She raised her only son, John, with the help of her sister, brother-in-law, and their daughter Emily. Unfortunately, in 1962 John was afflicted with the same kidney disease which had taken the lives of most of the men in his family. A new experimental procedure known as a kidney transplant offered some hope. However, finding a suitable organ donor was a substantial challenge. The word of a perfect match for John came literally at the last minute. It was only after the transplant, as both patients were recovering in ICU, did the family learn the donor was John's cousin, Emily.

The transplant was a success, and John lived another twelve years with his new kidney, and during this time, he fathered twin sons—Johnathan and James. Unfortunately, Emily passed away a year after the transplant from surgical complications.

Johnathan sent me a copy of a letter from his Aunt Emily, which is a wonderful addition to my growing shoebox collection. The letter was written to the twins at the time of their birth, in which she articulated her dreams for her nephews and the responsibility they had in carrying on the family legacy.

After reading the letter, I understand why it is important for them to honor her memory by sending flowers to the Mound Creek Cemetery each year—appropriately at Easter. Postscript:

Through my Shoebox search, I have learned that

Johnathan and James each have three children, including a girl named Emily. Both twins are urologists specializing in kidney disease. Moreover, in 1981 James was part of an international medical team that discovered a treatment for the rare hereditary disease which took the lives of their father, grandfather, and several other relatives.

## Preserving the Written Word / Preserving your History

Emily's inspiring letter to her nephews was written at the time of their birth. She had literally given her life for these boys, and it was obvious her message was something she hoped would shape and inspire their character and their lives.

In my Shoebox files, I have numerous copies of letters grandmothers wrote to a newborn grandchild at the time of their birth. These letters were given to the child's parents for safekeeping and to be presented to the child when they might be old enough to appreciate the significance of the letter and the heartfelt sentiment behind it. Many of these letters are now over a half-century old; however, they continue to inspire new generations who never knew the original author.

# The Gospel According to Fern

Recently, I found a forty-six-year-old letter in the shoebox which dispelled a lifetime of very unflattering impressions of my insufferable Uncle Fern.

The origin of his unusual name is unknown. Proving that truth is always better than fiction, Fern's loyal wife was named Fred (short for Frederica). Fern was a small-town fire-and-brimstone preacher who served several South Texas congregations throughout his life. A mandatory visit to his church was non-debatable when my family traveled to his region of the state.

The misery of attending Uncle Fern's church always began with my parent's extra scrutiny of my wardrobe and hygiene. Shoes were polished to perfection, the top button of my best shirt was uncomfortably fastened to accommodate my clip-on tie, and of course, every hair was held in place by that oil slick of a hair product known as Brylcreem.

An Uncle Fern service was steeped in tradition. There

were some old standard hymns, the passing of the collection plate, and then he got down to serious business. With a voice so powerful he could be heard in the next county, he began his Sunday rants about the evils of Satan's infiltration into our daily lives.

It was customary for him to call out any parishioner he felt was not toeing the line. I lived in constant fear I would be publicly humiliated for some unknown transgression. He once shamed the high school football star for wearing white socks to church, and he even called for the removal of the homecoming queen for wearing a form-fitting dress to her coronation. (He quickly dismissed as a "mere coincidence" that his morally superior daughter, Frankie, was runner-up that year.)

The uncompromising gospel, according to Fern, gave me plenty of ammunition to dub him as a narrow-minded jerk. Then I uncovered some shoebox letters which showed old Fern had a compassionate and even progressive side to him.

Several letters, written in 1972, hinted a calamity was brewing in the Central Texas town of Marlin over the subject of evolution being taught to the sophomore class, which included Fern's granddaughter, Francis. In one letter, Frankie sought guidance from her father about what argument she should make to the school board when demanding Francis' excusal from this class.

Fern lowered the decimal level of this debate when he wrote to Francis, encouraging her to attend the science class with an open and compassionate heart. In a three-page letter, he told his granddaughter, "In my opinion, science and religion are not opposed to each other." He also told her she should embrace science as the best way to uncover truths about ourselves and our world. Fern emphatically stated, "I have studied scientific facts about our universe for many years, and I always conclude the more science I study, the more in awe I am of the amazing creativity of our heavenly Creator."

Who would ever have thought the study of science would have softened the heart of fire-and-brimstone Fern while strengthening his already unshakable faith? While he wouldn't dare preach on this subject in his day, he would be so pleased that today many progressive churches are approaching the same subject and coming up with the same conclusions he hit on decades ago: science and faith can co-exist.

# Aunt Fred Stands By Her Man

"Stand by your man and show the world you love him—Keep giving all the love you can. Stand by your man."

*Stand by Your Man*
Co-written by Tammy Wynette and Billy Sherrill

When I introduced you to Uncle Fern, I portrayed to you a man who was rigid and unyielding. Well, he was a nice warmup to prepare you for Aunt Fred! Her lineage was filled with a long line of preacher's wives, so her fate was sealed even before she met and married Uncle Fern. Her "job" in life was to stand by and protect her man. Frequently, you would find Aunt Fred at church, and when she wasn't there, she dutifully presided over keeping a neat and clean home. Every desk, table, and knick-knack were dust-free and in their proper place. Dinner was served at 5:30 p.m. sharp, and God help her two children if they were even one minute late!

At all times, Aunt Fred waged her own personal battle against Satan, who, she feared, was trying to disrupt her morally superior existence. Mouths were washed out with soap, and neighborhood children were banned from her home for uttering vile words, such as "gosh darn," "for God's sake," and the unforgivable "holy cow." "Cows aren't holy! This is America, not India!" was one of her favorite reminders to the junior blasphemers. Satan had met his match in Aunt Fred.

One of her most memorable crusades involved keeping a vigilant eye on the town library, making sure the local citizens were protected from "Satan-inspired" literature. In a 1962 saved letter written to her sister, Thelma, she spoke triumphally of her efforts to get the city council to ban from the library "contemporary and historical smut" such as *Catcher in the Rye*, *The Fountainhead*, and *Uncle Tom's Cabin*. She also wrote in months to come, her focus would be on the removal of *East of Eden*, *Atlas Shrugged*, *The Lord of the Flies*, and the "worst of the worst," *The Power of Positive Thinking*, which she deemed "sacrilegious."

For Aunt Fred, it was not enough to just remove a book from the library or throw away items of questionable content. She was not satisfied unless they were permanently destroyed by fire.

Many homes in rural towns of the time had large, fifty-gallon barrels in the backyard used to burn trash. Aunt Fred used hers to burn books, Elvis Presley records, and even a copy of *Readers Digest Magazine* because the issue printed the word "vagina." *National Geographic* certainly didn't escape Aunt Fred's watchful eye because of its practice of frequently showing photos of scantily attired African men and women in their tribal costumes.

Aunt Fred's morally superior attitude would have probably labeled her the original "church lady" were it not for one minor incident. Unfortunately for her, one of her crusades went awry, and for a period, she earned the label of "The Porn Peddler of Pleasanton."

The infamous day started out with Aunt Fred at her sanctimonious best after she discovered a cache of *Playboy* magazines under her teenage son's bed. Armed with a can of kerosene and a stack of magazines, she headed to the trash barrel where she ripped out page after page of topless women and vulgar cartoons and tossed them into the blazing inferno. Her son's collection was significant, and she had to make several trips back into the house to retrieve all the loot. In her haste, she forgot to place the protective wire cover over the barrel to keep the burning paper from floating away.

When she returned to the fire, she discovered hundreds of partially burned pages of naked women had risen out of the can and drifted into the nearby high school baseball field.

Making matters worse, the boy's team had just taken the field for practice.

The morally upright, self-righteous Aunt Fred, feared and respected preacher's wife, was *horrified*. Fortunately, townsfolk offered her more grace than she might've given had the situation been reversed. Her friends and neighbors got a good laugh out of it, and she was the occasional butt of a good joke. But ultimately, the entire issue was mostly forgotten.

# Letter Written During the Flu Pandemic of 1919 Offers Advice for Today

During this unprecedented disruption of our lives due to the global pandemic, many positive human-interest stories have emerged as people try to help others. However, media outlets continued to report disheartening examples of extreme hoarding, blatant greed, and downright meanness of people trying to capitalize on this crisis.

Recently, a cousin shared with me a century-old letter written to her great-grandmother from her twin sister about how her small Texas community dealt with the horrible flu pandemic of 1919. The human kindness articulated in this inspiring letter contains many positive messages and examples that will help us get through our own pandemic.

*Writer's note: I am publishing this letter as written with misspelled words and all. Also, the date on the letter is illegible; however, it appears to be October 25, 1919. This was amid an influenza plague that killed an estimated fifty to one hundred million people worldwide.*

Dear Martha,

God bless us all. Bobby went to the mail today and I received all three of your sweet letters. We have been in quarantine for almost a month and just yesterday we got word that the plague had lifted. The immediate news is for the most part we were spared. Just a minor case here.

Everybody is still talking about why our town got hit so hard. Doc Bradly thinks it started at The Summer Festivel [sic]. The town square was filled with more people than ever before. Less than a week later Lucy Shelton lost her little Annie who was one of my third graders. Before it was over her two other children died and her mother also died. She had already lost her Elroy in a combine accident two years earlier. Bless her soul.

Looking at Lucy, I know what our daddy meant when he always said tragedies brings out the best in folks. When the plague hit Lucy had already done her winter canning mostly fig and peach preserves. When word got out lots of people were running out of food, she put them in smaller jars and placed um out by the street for people to take. With her family gone Lucy said she had no use for them and just wanted to share.

I guess you remember Mr. Jonas down on the corner who always gave us the vegtables [sic]. He is fighting in France but before he left, he got his huge fall garden in. His wife Cora got the word out for everyone to just come help themselves to whatever they needed. Bobby and I watched it from the kitchen window and just like at Lucy's everyone entered the garden one at a time and nobody took more than they needed. I understand the McShane's over on Sycamore did the same.

We were ordered to stay in our home with doors and windows shut though we did go out a little. Most of our news came from Billy Johnson who works for Sherriff Owens. Every three or four days he would leave a mason [sic] of kerosene or turpentine on the front steps. We were instructed to wipe everything down with it. The kitchen counter, the table and the floor. Doc Bradly said we also needed to constantly wash our hands with soap and hot hot water. We were good there because I had made my soap at the end of August. When Billy hollered through the door people were running out of soap, I got busy with all the Lye I had left over and just kept the batches coming. I had to cook it on the stove so I don't know if we will ever get the smell out. We boxed them up and

Billy delivered to folks who was out. I was just glad we could do something.

I have got to sign off now, but I just wanted to let you know we are blessed and okay.

All my love to you and Roy,

Milly

*(All grammar and spelling has been left unedited.)*

# Letter Written During the Flu Pandemic in 1919—Part 2

## "Grateful for God's Blessings"

Shortly after publishing my great Aunt Milly's letter on the Shoebox Chronicle Blog, a distant relative contacted me who also had a letter written by Milly to her great-grandmother living in Iowa. The letter, dated December 12, 1919, is extremely fragile, and parts of it are illegible. However, the letter is noteworthy enough to pass on as valuable in today's environment.

The first letter was written the day the quarantine was lifted, and it focused on basic survival and acts of human kindness during this period. This new letter was written several months later, focusing on lessons learned during quarantine and their efforts to define their "new normal" and find hope for the future.

Unlike Milly's first letter, the condition of this correspondence prevents me from publishing it completely as written; however, here are some of the salient points I was able to glean.

*Health update:*

All in all we got off better than most. Only Callie [seventeen-year-old daughter] got it, but her fever broke on the fourth day. Betty Stevenson, the mother of Adam who is Callie's betrothed didn't make it. He is a strong young man and I think he will be okay. His daddy is the preacher to the Methodists, so they got the faith. Although, I think it would be better if they were Baptist.

*Planning for the Future:*

Who knows what type of future any of our kids will have anymore? Before all this hit, there was so much promise. It looked like the war was winding down so Adam didn't have to worry about that.—Bobby and I so want Callie to finish high school and maybe even go to teacher's college. But I don't even know if our school will have enough students to re-open, and who knows how long Bobby will have his job. So, college will probably not be an option. That seems to suit Callie just fine.

However, before the school closed, she was showing some real aptitude for short-hand and was learning to type. Girls can make good money with those skills these days. Adam says he is hoping to go to technical college in Ft. Worth so it would be good if she could help make ends meet.

All Johnny [sixteen-year-old son] wants to do is farm, so I guess there will always be work there.

### *Quarantine Isolation:*

In a strange sort of way, being locked up with just the four of us for thirty-six days had some silver lines [sic]. Before the plague, Bobby was going to work at the Mercantile every morning before daylight and I had already fed the kids by the time he got home. During [illegible] harvest he also worked most Saturday's at least till mid-afternoon. Both of us were glad to spend more time together as a family before they all go off on their own. Bobby and Johnny must have played a thousand games of checkers and every afternoon I helped Callie make her wedding dress. It is a beautiful white eye-lit that she can wear for Easter or to other weddings if she adds a shawl with some color. We ran out of material and found enough decent cloth on Grandma Baker's old quilt to finish the belt.

Every evening we turned on the radio and listened to the news report. But it was always the same and we could hardly stand to listen to more news about all these deaths and crop failures. I got to where I would just go in the bedroom until it was over. If there is a comforting part in all this sadness it was that after supper, we would pass around the family Bible and each read a verse or two just like our daddy always did. I think this gave us all hope.

### Reopening Church:

The first Baptist Church reopened last Sunday. I didn't go but Bobby said it was less than half full. I don't know if it is because people are scared to go back out in public, or if it is just so many people have died. I guess we will know in a few weeks when we have Christmas services.

### Upcoming Christmas:

This was Martha and her families turn to come to us for Christmas, but we canceled all that. We are going to just be grateful for being alive. I have enough preserves left to make a peach pie and we may go out to daddy's old farm and see if we can catch one of the chickens to fry. They are just running free since we moved to town. You probably remember Ruth Hopps' daughter Karen. She never married and runs her momma's boarding house now. One of her boarders had to pay his room with a typewriter which she sold to me for twenty-five cents. The L sticks but Bobby is going to try to oil it and give it to Callie for Christmas and her birthday. I think she will love it because the school only had one machine and all the girls wanted to use it so Callie could never get the practice she wanted.

We moved Cassy, our milking cow, into town and she is about to drop any day. Hopefully, she will have a healthy [illegible] and we are going to give it to Jimmy. I am sure that will be his best Christmas ever.

*Conclusion:*

The letter closed with her customary optimistic hopes for the future and her longing to see distant family members. She included her never-ending praise for our Heavenly Creator and her grateful heart for God's tender blessings.

*(All grammar and spelling has been left unedited.)*

# There Is a Family Bible on the Table

"There is a family Bible on the table. Its pages worn and hard to read. But the family Bible on the table will ever be my key to memories."

*The Family Bible*
Music and Lyrics by Willy Nelson

Growing up in my home, and in every relatives' home I visited in my youth, there was always a worn and well-read Bible either on a bedside table or near the primary family gathering place. The Bibles were viewed as holy ground, and I never dared touch them.

Recently, I ran head-on into an issue that dramatically displayed, yet again, why modern technology is eroding a tradition as sacred as the family Bible.

The day was exciting and filled with anticipation as a most admired friend and a man of great faith was being sworn-in to office as a district judge. As I was preparing to go to the ceremony, I received a call from the judge-elect. In a rather disjointed voice, he asked if I could bring one of my Bible's to the swearing-in for him to use when taking the oath of office. "Of course," I agreed. But the situation begged the question, "What's wrong with your Bible?" His answer stunned me when he sheepishly admitted they could not find it, and what more—he was not sure they even owned one. He then defended this shortcoming by saying he had four Bible apps on his cellphone. My sarcasm was not well received when I suggested his wife just hold up his phone and let him take the oath on it.

Make no mistake, I love my Bible app. It provides quick and easy access to scripture in multiple translations. I can take it places not convenient to lug my personal Bible. But convenience is not a replacement for a well-worn and well-read family treasure.

I am so glad my family chose to save all our old Bibles and have passed them down through the generations. In addition to recording a family's history of births, deaths, and weddings at the front of the Bible, these treasures tell us so much more about the person who read them and the history they were living. As the Willie Nelson song says, the family Bible is "the key to memories." It is these memories that connect the dots of our history through the generations.

In reading old family Bibles, I get a glimpse of the thoughts and values that guided the owner. Although common today, in my grandparents' and great-grandparents' times, it was sacrilege to write or underline words in a Bible, so they stuffed them with letters, photos of loved ones, birth announcements, and faded newspaper clips of weddings and obituaries. Even today, these Bibles are literally museums of a family's history.

My grandfather's Bible is a crumbled mass of aged paper. But it is packed with handwritten notes on scraps of paper about what specific verses meant to him. These notes are the only thing I have of his writings as he talks about how God's word helped him through crop failures, death of a child, and his struggles providing food for his family during the Great Depression. He often concluded his notes with words about how God never disappoints and always provides. This old message from a family Bible is as relevant today as ever before. However, the question of our time remains: How do you pass down your cell phone to the next generation?

## Preserving the Written Word /
## Preserving Your History

I have a cousin who has carefully saved family Bibles from her parents, grandparents, and in-laws. She has placed in her last will and testament specific instructions on whom she wants to have each Bible upon her death. In the front of each Bible, she has written a personal note articulating why she has entrusted this specific person with this family treasure. The letters include family history and stories about the original owner of the Bible. She even makes references to special verses that remind her of the owner. Whenever possible, she has included photos of the ancestor, their obituary, and life altering events which may have shaped this person's life and caused them to seek refuge and comfort in their own family Bible.

After publishing the family Bible story on my social media blog, a reader posted this comment: "After reading your Shoebox Chronicles about the family Bible, I had a deep desire to share my faith and love for Jesus with my children, and yet to be born grandchildren and great-grandchildren. I purchased a journal Bible which included space for me to write my thoughts, prayers, and learnings God has blessed me with over the years. I hope to finish it before I, too, go to heaven. It's so fun!! Thank you for inspiring me to leave my legacy."

# A New Spin on an Old Holiday Tradition

For generations, a holiday tradition in my family was to string a wire across the fireplace mantel to display much-anticipated Christmas cards. The cards would fill the mailbox in the days leading up to Christmas as loved ones touched base with friends and family. Most of the cards came with hand-written correspondence of annual family updates. I remember my parents sitting down each evening to read the cards as a rite of the holidays.

The notes were usually hand-written and heartfelt. With one exception. Our beloved Aunt Beth always typed out a long letter highlighting her family's "too-good-to-be-true" annual accomplishments. She would mimeograph (a lost term for a bad copy job) the letter in mass to send out to all us—less fortunate souls. It was amusing to read about how her husband received yet another promotion, their son continued to be at the top of his class, her daughter was once again voted most popular in school, and Beth stayed busy going to meetings and decorating the new house. (I think every family has an Aunt Beth.)

During a recent annual Christmas Eve gathering, several cousins shared some of their family's old cards that have survived through the years. In reading these cards, we all learned so much about our family legacy. We roared with laughter at a letter from Aunt Beth's sister where she spilled the beans that the perfect picture her sister painted of her "wonderful life" may have been a bit exaggerated. Or, at least, omitting information that included the daughter's "shotgun" wedding and an embezzlement conviction by her philandering husband. We were not laughing at Aunt Beth and her woes—just celebrating more family trials, triumphs, and rich histories.

The wire across the mantel for holiday cards is a long-gone tradition. Most modern Christmas cards are glossy postcards with a pre-printed message or an impersonal post on Facebook. This is not all bad because, thanks to social media, we don't have to wait for an annual card to get important updates from friends and family. The problem is today's cards are easily trashed as "insignificant" or discarded with a touch of a "delete" button.

While Christmas messaging may no longer be the answer, we need to look for ways to preserve our family heritage, and the written word remains paramount.

In my own small trove of family mementos, stuffed between Boy Scout merit badges and baseball participation trophies, are three letters written to my brother and me from our mother dated on the last day of the decade for the 1970s, 1980s, and 1990s. She wanted to mark the end of each decade with some personal thoughts and memories. While her dedication to family and faith was unquestioned, she went on to list other important items in her life over the previous ten years. The list included her favorite rescue dog(s), favorite book and movie, memorable trips, noteworthy milestones, and personal accomplishments. Looking forward, she was optimistic about all the fast-paced opportunities my brother and I would enjoy in coming years. She concluded each letter with some spiritual advice encouraging us to seek God's will in all ways.

## Preserving the Written Word /
## Preserving Your History

The first of my mom's letters, reflecting on personal memories of the 1970's, turns forty years old this year as we celebrate the end of another decade. This type of milestone is an excellent way to start a new tradition of your own by reaching out to family members with a written correspondence. Your memory may just end up in someone's family treasures that inspires and educates future generations.

"Freedom is never more than one generation away from extinction. We did not pass it to our children in the bloodstream. It must be fought for, protected, and handed on for them to do the same, or one day we will spend our sunset years telling our children and our children's children what it was once like in the United States where men were free."

President Ronald Reagan
Memorial Day Address,
Arlington National Cemetery

# Remembering Well—A Memorial Day Tribute

A recent flight delay leaving Washington, DC, gave me a couple of rare free hours. I had a choice to see several of the new monuments, a new museum, or just to visit favorite landmarks in this wonderful and uniquely American city. I opted for Arlington National Cemetery.

I have been to this historic landmark more times than I can remember, but every time I have been emotionally impacted by the scene of six hundred and twenty-four acres of rolling hills marked with over four hundred thousand white grave markers of American soldiers. This trip was especially impactful as preparations were underway for Memorial Day remembrances. Volunteers were already positioning crates of small American flags around the property so that other volunteers can place them on each grave as a Memorial Day tradition.

Memorial Day is a time we as a nation honor Americans who died in military service. Unfortunately, the real purpose of this day seems to get lost among announcements of super blowout sales at the local mall and the bedlam associated with the start of summer vacations.

In my shoebox files is a large envelope of letters titled "Norvin Davis letters." Previously, I only knew that I had a second cousin named Norvin, who died in World War II at the age of twenty-two. But from these letters, I learned about his dreams, his philosophy about his own death, how he died, and why he was honored to make the ultimate sacrifice if necessary.

At West Point, his classmates nicknamed him "Smiley," and he was considered the ultimate optimist and team leader. He loved to fish, was an avid horseman, and signed up for every volunteer military competition with his fellow cadets. Norvin and his roommate "Saint" took early graduation to enter the war effort where "Saint" went to the European theatre and Norvin to the Pacific. The letters passed between them as fast as time and distance would allow.

I learned my cousin dreamed of getting married and starting a family. But he did have his priorities, and the first thing he was going to do when the war was over was to get his "very own big yellow dog." In one of the last letters to "Saint," he wrote of dying, "I am not afraid of dying, but the hard part is knowing the ones I love will suffer." Norvin would have been comforted knowing his academy classmates and the entire squadron he commanded devoted much of their post-war lives to comforting my aunt and uncle with calls, personal visits, and all those letters.

In one condolence letter, Lt. Gen. O. W. Griswold, Commander of the XIV Corps, wrote fondly of Norvin. He concluded by saying, "I have no doubt we will win this war. What concerns us all after that is whether the people themselves can win and keep the peace. If this can be done, I feel that our American boys who fell in battle will have as their memorial the greatest monument ever built by the human race."

I am grateful these letters were preserved as an important part of my family and our nation's history. Philosopher George Santayana once wrote, "Those who cannot remember the past are condemned to repeat it."

It is vital to the future of our nation that we take time on Memorial Day to remember all soldiers who died in military service. They shaped our national history. We cannot just honor our dead—we must learn from them. The future of this great nation depends on it.

# Family History Uncovers Holocaust Ties

I have always known my family history was connected to World War II Germany, and some family members were directly impacted by the Holocaust. The early origins of our family history during this horrific time were documented in a letter written by my great Aunt Gertrude from Heidelberg, Germany, to American family members in Ohio. Part of this letter gave an update on her son Hetrick and his family who were living in Berlin at the time. Hetrick had recently sent his mother a letter informing her of recent events in Berlin. It is my understanding Hedrick's original letter is now part of a Holocaust archive in Bad Arolsen, Germany.

One historical significance of this letter is its date—November 13, 1938. Only days after what would later be known as Kristallnacht (Crystal Night or the Night of Broken Glass). Actions on this date were one of the first public steps toward Adolf Hitler's "Final Solution." In her letter, Gertrude tells of Hetrick's eyewitness account of the night of terror where Jewish-owned businesses, synagogues, and homes were rampaged by Hitler youth gangs. One heart-wrenching part of the letter described how Hetrick ran to the home of a friend in law enforcement to get help for a neighbor whose bakery was being devastated. Hetrick saw the officer inside his home, but he refused to answer his door.

Prior to this incident, Hetrick, his wife, Mariam, and their young daughter Davida lived a low-key life in Berlin, where he and his wife were professors at a local college. Hetrick was an active member of the German Lutheran Church and a decorated World War I veteran. Miriam was Jewish. Days after Crystal Night, they left Berlin for what they hoped would be a safer environment in their hometown of Heidelberg near the Swiss border.

At some point, Miriam and Davida fled Germany and crossed into Switzerland to live on the swine farm of a very long-time loyal family friend. It was also no longer safe to be considered an "intellectual" in Germany, so Hetrick left his teaching position at the University of Heidelberg and took a job working for the state-run railroad.

Life was both harsh and challenging for Miriam and Davida in Switzerland. Hitler sympathizers were constantly threatening to expose their hiding place, and their benefactor endured blackmail to keep them safe. During this time, Aunt

Gertrude wrote a letter to her American family members, pleading for financial help for her daughter-in-law and granddaughter.

Gertrude's letter was extremely risky because she was sending it from Nazi-controlled Germany to Americans, soliciting financial aid for Jews hiding in Switzerland. Hetrick smuggled the letter to Belgium, where he clandestinely placed it in the hands of a trusted ally who was traveling on diplomatic credentials. The letter was eventually mailed from England.

The letter contained specific instructions on how to get money (cash) to the farmer shielding, Miriam and Davida. Mail was often intercepted by the Nazis, adding stress to an already inflamed situation. Detailed directions followed about never mentioning the names of our relatives and to note the money was simply to be used to help his pig farm.

The direness of the situation resulted in a host of letters being written back and forth between family members living in Ohio, Iowa, and Texas about Aunt Gertrude's desperate pleas. In later years, a cousin started collecting old family mementos and writings that included many of these World War II letters.

Unfortunately, a well-intended, yet misguided relative from Texas persuaded my cousin to destroy all letters referencing financial aid for Miriam and Davida. Her rationale was the reference of aid for Jewish relatives fleeing the Holocaust, guised as money for a "pig farm" could be misconstrued as anti-Semitic.

The only record in our family archives about the existence of these letters was contained in a saved letter my misguided relative wrote to her sister, Aunt Fred, informing her she persuaded her niece to burn the letters. This letter did not make it clear if she was concerned about being viewed as anti-Semitic or if she did not want people to know of our Jewish lineage. Sadly, this sole surviving letter did not offer me enough information to allow me to go public with a story about my American family aiding relatives during the Holocaust.

This situation came full circle when I recently was introduced to a distant cousin, Gretchen, living in Ohio. In 1978, she spent a year living in Germany as an exchange student. During this time, she contacted the small remnants of our German family. They ultimately put her in contact with the eighty-four-year-old farmer living in Lucerne, Switzerland, who had hidden Miriam and Davida during the war.

This farmer confirmed the cash from the United States, which came regularly to his post office box from my family members, was a total godsend during the war. He mentioned several of our now departed relatives by name, and he even saved a couple of old envelopes as part of his stamp collection.

I am so grateful my cousin kept a detailed journal about her studies abroad which she has forwarded to me. It is this saved journal that allows me to make this post about a little-known part of my family history.

# Family Holocaust Ties (Part 2)

## We Have a Tree in Israel

"The fruits of the olive tree only gives its oil when pressed, and the Children of Israel are only brought back to the right path by travails."

Talmud Offerings 23

In the waning days of World War II, my uncle Hetrick died of natural causes. With her husband now dead and her own family decimated by the Holocaust, Miriam made the difficult decision to not return to Germany. She and Davida briefly lived in Zurich, Switzerland, with her primary desire to legally immigrate to Palestine.

Miriam was deeply impacted by the historical plight of her ancestry. After experiencing the same burden during the Holocaust, she wanted to see her daughter grow up surrounded by people of the Jewish faith in the safest possible place. Palestine would at least offer Davida a fighting chance of not suffering the generational fate of her family before her.

The post-war trail of Miriam and Davida is faint; only a couple of letters connect the dots of their journey. Evidently, at some point, their efforts to legally obtain permanent asylum in the Middle East did not materialize, and they began their migration using fake passports provided to them by a Zionist[1] organization operating in Switzerland.

In a letter written to Aunt Gertrude in 1947, Miriam notified her in-laws she and Davida had been interned in Cyprus by British forces. There was great irony in the fact that Miriam and Davida spent four years avoiding Nazi concentration camps during the war yet ended up in one controlled by Great Britain as part of British efforts to manage immigration of post-war Europeans to Palestine.

There was no known contact from Miriam after this letter. In November 1948, a letter was written to Aunt Gertrude by a British nurse, Tilly Brannon (or Branigan), who had befriended Miriam during her Cyprus incarceration. The brief letter informed Gertrude of her daughter-in-law's death as the result of a chronic respiratory condition exacerbated by the harsh conditions in the camp. The letter said Davida thrived in a special camp set up for children, mostly orphans, where she attended school for the first time in her life. Tilly described how Miriam met with Davida often and worked valiantly to instill in her the importance of carrying on the family legacy in their Jewish homeland of Israel.

The letter explained how Miriam died, almost euphoric; her mission had been accomplished. Only weeks before her death, she received a postcard from British authorities informing her Davida was part of a small group of children who had legally arrived in Palestine for resettlement. Moreover, Miriam was buoyed by constant news the formation of the nation of Israel was quickly becoming a reality.

Tilly's letter has not been saved. Its existence was verified in a 1949 letter Gertrude wrote to her sister-in-law in the United States in which she mentioned the fate of Miriam and Davida. (Fortunately, Gertrude's letter has been saved.)

Two generations of my family conducted extensive searches in Israel looking for Davida. All efforts were futile as it was a very chaotic time for the fledging nation where over two hundred and fifty thousand settlers had moved in 1949 alone. Also, most Jewish children adopted Hebrew names upon arrival in Palestine, and without knowing her new name, a search was almost impossible.

In 1986, one of my Jewish American cousins, Hannah Nusbaum, lived in Israel for a year. During this time, she continued the search for Davida or any family remnants she might have. The only concrete reference she found was the existence of a British nurse named Tilly Brannigan. The description of her and the time frame of her humanitarian efforts in Cyprus were aligned with the person mistakenly identified by Gertrude as Tilly Brannon.

Before leaving Israel, Hannah was joined by other American family members making their first pilgrimage to this country. During this trip, they planted a fig tree outside Jerusalem on the banks of the Jordan River as a solemn remembrance honoring Miriam and Davida.

### Preserving the Written Word /
### Preserving Your History

Fortunately, Hannah and Gretchen kept detailed journals/diaries about their pilgrimages to Germany and Israel. These diaries, though decades old, were never discarded and provide rich detail about my family history.

Diaries have been a very important part of my family. Evidently, the tradition started by a wonderful distant relative who was inspired by the book *The Diary of Ann Frank* which she read as a young adult. From that time on, she gave every niece who graduated from high school a copy of the famous book and a diary so that family members could journal their new life experiences.

Diaries may not immediately be a welcome gift at graduation. However, they certainly have greater longevity than cash, gift cards, or the latest technological advancement which is usually obsolete before it is even used.

You cannot go back and change the beginning, but you can start where you are and change the ending."

C. S. Lewis,
Author

# Question Authority

In my parent's photo album, there is an interesting photo of my distant cousin Rusty. The photo was of Rusty standing behind a very packed Volkswagen bug in our driveway. He had shoulder-length red hair, was wearing a tie-dye tee-shirt, and was defiantly giving the peace sign. On the bumper of his car was a popular anti-war message of the time which read: "question authority."

I barely remember Rusty. He was six years older than me, the only child of my cousin Sally and her husband, Clyde. We saw each other at family get-togethers and exchanged Christmas cards regularly up until 1968. Suddenly, all correspondence and visits stopped.

Intrigued by what could be a family mystery, I began an internet search. After numerous dead ends, I finally struck paydirt when I spoke to their neighbor who told me the very reclusive Sally had moved to Tampa, Florida, after Clyde's death of lung cancer in 1991. I asked her about Rusty, and she said nobody had seen him since he left for college.

I finally located Sally, who was now ninety years old and living with Rusty's son and family in Clearwater, Florida. She was happy to hear from me but reluctant to visit about her family history and, specifically, Rusty. After reading some of *The Shoebox Chronicles*, she called me and said she would like her family's story to be added to the collection.

She shared with me a dark tale of how Rusty turned eighteen at the height of the Vietnam War. He entered the University of North Texas as a music major but spent most of his freshman year engaged in anti-war protests. He quickly flunked out of school, which resulted in him losing his college deferment from the military draft. Upon receiving his draft notice in 1968, and with his mother's blessing, Rusty went on the lam. In fact, we both surmised the photo my parents had of Rusty was probably taken in the very early days of his life as a fugitive.

In 1969, with federal authorities closing in on him, and facing a multi-year prison sentence, Rusty secretly crossed the border into Canada, where he joined tens of thousands of other young American men seeking political asylum to avoid fighting in Vietnam. For over eight years, he lived in exile in Montreal, Canada.

Sally said she and Clyde stayed totally quiet about Rusty's actions because they did not want to betray his location or to be dragged into the great war debate that was polarizing the nation. Each night she watched the evening news and was just glad her only son was safe as she heard reports of mounting death tolls amid the atrocities of the war.

The situation was especially hard on Clyde. His family had a long history of distinguished military service, and he seemed embarrassed and ashamed by the path his son had taken. Making matters worse was the fact that Clyde's brother, James, was a highly decorated Colonel in the Army working at the Pentagon. Rubbing salt in the wound was the issue of James's all too perfect son Bradley (named after World War II commander Omar Bradley), who received his military commission upon graduating from Texas A & M University and was serving his second tour of duty in Vietnam.

Sally sent me copies of three letters that personalized the impact the war and its aftermath had on her family.

The first letter was from James to Clyde, and it was written while Rusty was in exile. In the letter, James harshly criticized Rusty, bragged incessantly about Bradley, and went to great lengths to defend the American war effort. He did, however, offer to use his influence in Washington, DC, to get Rusty "back on track." Rusty and Sally politely rejected the offer because it included mandatory military service or jail time.

Rusty finally returned to the United States in 1977 after President Jimmy Carter issued a pardon for all draft dodgers.

After years of weathering the frigid temperatures of Montreal, he settled in sunny Florida, where he married and had a son.

The second letter was from Rusty to his parents. In the undated letter, he said, "I refuse to apologize for my actions during the war. However, I am only now beginning to realize how much of a toll it took on you. In saving my life, I am afraid I may have destroyed yours. Dad, Aunt Jayne was here recently, and she tells me after I left, you started smoking again and how you spent most evenings sitting alone in the dark living room drinking whiskey. And mom, she tells me you quit your garden club and bridge group and never even returned to your beloved church. For the pain and suffering I have caused you both, I will not be able to forgive myself."

Unfortunately, Rusty never really recovered from an intravenous drug habit he began while in Canada, and he died at the age of fifty-six from the effects of long-term alcohol and drug abuse.

Bradley returned from the war honored as a hero with two Purple Hearts and a Bronze Star for bravery. He married and had two children. Unfortunately, a few years after his return, he became obsessed and haunted by the Vietnam experience, and this sent him into a very dark place from which he never recovered. He spent most of his adult life in and out of veterans' hospitals, abusing drugs, and joining other veterans trying to cope with what they saw and did during the war. He died at the age of fifty-one, and though his cause of death was not disclosed, it was generally suspected to be a suicide.

The third letter was written from James to Sally after Rusty's death. In the letter, he wrote at length about some of his actions during the war. He said the biggest regret of his life was lobbying members of the US Congress in support of Tonkin Gulf Resolution, which greatly escalated the American war effort. He said he never questioned the validity of the information he espoused, which turned out to be totally fabricated.

James concluded his letter by writing, "This fall, Beth and I rekindled an old tradition of spending our Saturday mornings in what I call 'scrounging,' and she calls 'treasuring hunting' at garage sales in the Northern Virginia and DC area. We had not done this since Bradley's death, and I think we both thought it was time to resume some sort of normalcy in our lives. I went on these excursions because I just enjoyed the special time with Beth. I never intended to purchase anything; however, at the last sale of the season, I found a treasure for the bargain-basement price of fifteen cents. I brought it home, reframed it, and hung it on a wall in my office alongside announcements of all my military promotions, letters of commendation, and numerous shadowboxes of medals. I am, for the most part, very proud of my military service; however, my recent addition to this wall sums up the final and most important lesson I learned from a forty-eight-year career. The treasure is a quote from Benjamin Franklin which reads, 'It is the responsibility of every citizen to question authority.'

"I think this statement represents the valuable truth this nation gleaned from Vietnam. An entire generation will probably have to die off before we are completely free of the mistakes made by so many of the era. Those who served, those who ran, those of us who blindly carried out orders without question.

"I guess Vietnam has made us a better nation, but what a price we all paid. What a terrible price."

Preserving the Written Word /
Preserving Your History

"Pictures never die, they just keep on smiling eternally."

From the song: *I'll Go on Living*
Music and lyrics by Darrell H. Murphy

It is not enough just to save those photo albums—had my mom not saved a photo of Rusty and written the inscription—"*Rusty—1968*" I would have never followed up or uncovered this important story about the impact of a dark period in our family and nations history. Preserving the written word does not always mean a lot of words. In this case, just a date and a name did the trick. Of course, pictures say a thousand words so go a step beyond your cell phone to permanently archive your family treasurers and history.

"We must scrupulously guard the civil rights and civil liberties of all citizens, whatever their background. We must remember that any oppression, any injustice, any hatred, is a wedge designed to attack our civilization."

Franklin Roosevelt,
President of the United States

# Old Letters Show Family's Civil Rights Origins

"Don't just pretend to love others. Really love them. Hate what is wrong. Hold tightly to what is good" (Romans 12:9, NLT).

My second Cousin Timothy (Tim) appeared to be the rising star in his family. He was the youngest of three brothers who, like their father and grandfather, were union workers at the Houston Ship Channel. In 1952, he showed real promise of improving his lot in life by enlisting in the Army, where he hoped to eventually take advantage of the GI Bill and go to college.

Tim served a year overseas during the Korean War, where he moved up in rank, saw significant combat duty, and returned home injury-free. Unfortunately, he was not so fortunate during a brief pre-discharge stay in Seattle, Washington, where a motorcycle accident landed him in the hospital for a few weeks.

While hospitalized, Tim fell in love with his beautiful nurse, Hattie. They were married by a justice of the peace before returning to his home and family in the blue-collar community near Houston, Texas. The only problem was it was 1955. Tim was white, Hattie was black, and they were returning to the highly segregated deep south in the waning days of Jim Crow era.

Letters flew back and forth between distressed family members. Well-meaning Aunt Fred wrote a letter to Tim's mom with what she thought was a workable solution. She wrote, "We have met Hattie, and she is an absolutely lovely Christian woman. I am just so sorry this situation has caused you so much heartache. However, I just may have a solution. Hattie is very light-skinned. I have heard a lot of negro women are growing their hair long and straightening it with an iron. Hattie could do this and dye her hair blond, and I am sure she could pass for white." She added, "Rumor has it this is what singer Dinah Shore does." (Unfortunately for Aunt Fred, her letter has survived and been the source of family amusement for years.)

Needless to say, the suggestion was politely rejected. While the family may have been divided internally, publicly, they were fierce defenders of Tim and Hattie. The situation came to a head when Tim's oldest brother, Nathan, ended up in the hospital with stitches and a broken nose after a bar-room fight defending his family's honor.

This was the last straw for Tim and Hattie. Tim left a letter on his parent's door apologizing for the pain he had caused his family. To alleviate any more family discourse, he and Hattie had decided to move to the northeast, where they hoped to find a more accepting environment to raise their unborn child.

By all accounts, Tim and Hattie flourished in Detroit, Michigan. Tim moved up in middle management at Ford Motor Company, and Hattie continued working in healthcare. Their only child was the first of our family to graduate from college, and he was even elected to the city council of his suburban Detroit city.

There was very little contact between Tim and his family after he and Hattie left Texas. However, this was the start of our family's long-time involvement in the civil rights movement. Tim's mother, father, and both brothers participated in a civil rights march in 1967 lead by Dr. Martin Luther King. Also, his mother worked a picket line protesting the "whites only" cafeteria inside Houston's City Hall.

All my life I have been very proud of our family's outspoken involvement in civil rights issues. It is very gratifying that a few old letters from Tim's family have introduced us to the origins of this lifetime and life-altering cause.

After touring pioneer America in 1832, legendary French historian and author Alexis de Tocqueville wrote:

"And if anyone asks me what I think the chief cause of the extraordinary prosperity and growing power of this nation, I should answer that it is due to the superiority of their women."

# Honoring America's Pioneer Women

As I continued reading through my family history from the shoebox of letters, I identified hundreds of correspondences I considered throwing away. They were simple letters written to and from my grandmother and her three sisters between 1909 and 1973.

The content of the letters was nothing remarkable at first glance. Written on inexpensive, recycled note paper, the letters contained mundane family updates, gardening tips, an occasional recipe, and always talk about the weather. What occurred to me was, what was not in the letters is what made them so special. Let me explain further.

Never in these letters was there a complaint, an ill word spoken of anyone, or a longing for a different life. It was not because they didn't have reason to moan. The first decades of all their lives were laced with difficult daily labors and great tragedies. Such was the fate of the American pioneer woman.

My grandmother and her sisters' first homes contained no telephones, electricity, or indoor plumbing. These letters— their only means of long-distance communication – tell the story of the last of a breed of woman who shaped the values, work ethic, and moral fiber of our nation.

My maternal grandmother, Mrs. Eula May Davis (Gram), was the epitome of the pioneer women of her time. Born in 1889, she worked endlessly to help her husband scrape out a meager existence for their family. Except for a ten-minute quiet time with her Bible after lunch, I never saw her rest. There were always cows to milk, eggs to collect, vegetable gardens to water, and of course, endless meals to prepare and clothes to wash. Even though she outlived her husband and three of her four children, she considered herself to be a blessed woman.

None of the pioneer women in these letters seemed to have any regrets about their lives. Each hardship they fought through brought them closer to their dreams of a better life for their children and grandchildren. I remember seeing Gram absolutely glow with happiness when she saw the educational opportunities afforded me as a young boy. Only now do I understand it was a feeling of complete and total satisfaction that all her struggles were worth it.

Her simple philosophy about life was summed up in a recently discovered letter she wrote in 1972 to my mom about her own funeral. Her only request was that her favorite Bible verse, Philippians 4:19, should be read at the service. She wanted her last message to be that in times of adversity, "God is adequately sufficient to supply all your needs." This was the mantra that brought her great comfort on this earth as she now joyously reaps her heavenly reward.

*Writer's note: Part 2 of this blog titled "Pioneer Spirit Lives Today" highlights how modern women have built on the past lessons of their ancestors to keep the American Pioneer spirit alive today. Letters written in more recent years show the conveniences of life may have changed, but the challenges have not.*

# Honoring America's Pioneer Women (Part 2)

## The Pioneer Spirit Lives Today

My cousin Joyce is about as close to a sister I have. We are the same age, went to the same college, and she even married my college roommate, Tray. She is a modern woman of her time. She effectively manages her home and family, a successful professional career while keeping up with the cutting-edge trends of the day. Like me, she took an interest in our family history and was inspired by the hardships and attitudes of past generations, especially when it came to the women in our family.

Her personal shoebox collection contains a recently shared letter from our Aunt Thelma, highlighting the family progression of the women from our ancestral past.

The letter was written to Joyce after a 1998 visit by Aunt Thelma, who was making a seven hundred mile solo trip from

Waco, Texas, to visit family in Montgomery, Alabama. Her frugal-minded itinerary called for her to stay with relatives along the way to avoid expensive motels, and this included an overnight stay at Joyce's home in Houston, Texas.

Joyce was conflicted about the visit. She wanted to see her aunt, whom she dearly loved and had not seen in a long time. She was also amazed a lady in her late eighties would undertake such a challenging road trip which included a barrage of Houston freeways, long patches of deserted rural roads, and a pass through the sin city of the south: New Orleans. The conflict came with the anticipated, and almost certain, chronic criticism of virtually every aspect of Joyce's modern life.

Paramount on Joyce's mind was Thelma's prior visit three years earlier when she and her sister, Aunt Fred, attended the funeral of Joyce's mother. The visit had its uncomfortable moments when both aunts gave her a glare of disapproval that Joyce's designer dress was not traditional "funeral black." Moreover, evidently, the dress showed a touch of cleavage, which Aunt Fred tried to remedy by slipping her a safety pin during the service.

The situation only got worse at the post-funeral cocktail reception at Joyce and Tray's home. The aunts were discovered sipping hot coffee in the sweltering Texas heat in the backyard. When Joyce approached them about coming inside where there's air conditioning, Thelma quickly got to the root of the problem when she said, "Fred and I were just reminiscing about how things have changed. In your grandmother's day, she would never allow anyone to bring liquor into her home." Fred weighed in by adding, "If any of the menfolk wanted to engage in that type of sinful behavior, they had to take it outside behind the barn. Now here we are just two generations advanced, and the reprobates are living it up in the house while the church folks are relegated to the backyard."

So, with a bit of trepidation, Joyce welcomed Thelma, who arrived two hours early with her signature homemade apple pie in hand. Joyce was determined not to yield to pressure by maintaining archaic moral traditions of her mother's generation. Her only exception was she didn't want to address the uncertain future of her marriage with her aunt, so she instructed her two teenage children to go along with her story that Tray was on a three-day business trip.

The twelve-hour visit almost went off without incident. The children were well behaved and even carved out twenty minutes to enjoy their aunts' company over take-out Chinese which was served on paper plates around the coffee table. The elegant twelve-chair dining room table was not an option as it doubled as a "catch-all" for family papers, unopened mail, old newspapers, and anything in print put aside to read at a more convenient time. Thelma gave the cluttered mess a disapproving once-over then moved on to be dazzled hearing of the children's college options, sports accomplishments, and expert use of chopsticks.

Thelma went to bed early and expressed her desire to be on the road by 6 a.m. the next morning. This gave Joyce time to work in a thirty-minute jog before leading Thelma through the neighborhood to a freeway short-cut. When Joyce left the house at 5:00 a.m., she noticed the lights were on in the guest room, so everything was on schedule.

When Joyce returned to her home, Thelma was packed and standing by her car. Joyce rushed into the house to retrieve her car keys, where she noticed the guest sheets were already in the dryer, the dining room table was not only cleaned of all papers but re-set with breakfast dishes, and there was a breakfast casserole in the oven.

While mildly annoyed by her aunt's antics, Joyce held her tongue. She guided her aunt onto the freeway, and she watched with amusement and a lot of admiration as Thelma drove away, hugging the inside lane of a mega-freeway at a roaring speed of thirty miles an hour.

A few weeks later, Joyce received a large packet in the mail from Thelma. The thickness of the mailing led Joyce to conclude the "thank you" letter would be laced with criticism, disappointments, and judgments. Wanting to avoid the inevitable for a few days, she finally crawled into bed one evening with the letter and a large glass of wine, ready to face her comeuppance!

To her surprise, Thelma's rambling letter began with a sincere thank you for the hospitality Joyce had shown her on her recent trip. She even apologized for taking liberties with cleaning off the dining-room table. But she pointed out the items she threw away were expired coupons, year-old invitations to Christmas parties, and school permission slips for events past. She did say, "I hope you noticed I stacked what looked like important papers such as current bills, college applications, and a letter from your divorce attorney on your desk." She wrote, "By the way, I didn't think Tray was just on a short business trip when I noticed his underwear drawer was completely empty."

She expressed sorrow that the marriage might be over; however, she used the situation to express pride in Joyce's generational progression. She commented, "I know divorces can be tough. But so is staying in a bad marriage for many years because of financial necessity. In my generation, many women endured unthinkable situations simply because they had no way of making a living if they left. Those who did leave lived compromised lifestyles while their husbands simply went on without missing a beat, financially or otherwise."

Thelma praised Joyce for having her own financial security brought on by career opportunities not available to previous generations. Joyce then noted the inclusion of several letters written to her mother almost a century ago from her grandmother. There were other letters from Joyce's mother to her cousins, Thelma and Fred.

She referenced the old correspondences as a way for Joyce to see just how far she had come, noting, "All of our past women would be so proud of you and, even if I don't agree with some of your decisions, I, too, am very proud." She concluded, "The comforts may improve from generation to generation, but the hard efforts are still just as challenging for women. But look how far you have come. And gosh almighty, the opportunities you have given your daughter. She tells me she wants to be an astronaut, no less. That won't be easy, but us ladies have never shied away from hard work."

As Joyce placed Thelma's letter along with the letters from past generations in a drawer for safekeeping, she realized she would one day share them with her daughter and hopefully grandchildren. Prior to Thelma's imparting her generational wisdom, Joyce thought of her chaotic life as just an endless stream of exhausting to-do lists and a never-ending balancing act between family and career obligations.

By connecting with women in her past, she could now identify with their pioneer legacy. Her first ancestors came to America in the early 1800s. They could not read, write, or speak English. Now one of their descendants has the realistic opportunity to take the family legacy all the way into outer space.

"You are our living link to the past. Tell your grandchildren the story of struggles waged at home and abroad, of sacrifices freely made for freedom's sake. And tell them your own story as well, because every American has a story to tell."

President George H.W. Bush,
1990 State of the Union Address

# Wisdom

"Every time an old person dies, it's like a library burns down."

Alex Haley,
Author of *Roots*

I have dozens of letters written between my grandmother and her sisters over the years, but nothing written between the men in our family. Proving the age-old problem, men don't write. What was true three generations ago is still true today.

While men may not write, they were certainly written about. As my grandfather and his peers aged, there was plenty written about them as their spouses and children worried about how they were handling the aging process. Letters are filled with statements like: "It is sad to see him this way. He just longs for the days when he was more useful." Or "Your father just sits around wishing he still had value." And a letter from my grandmother to my mother said, "Your father feels his purpose here on earth is over, and he is just a bother to everyone now."

Older men may not still be able to plow a field, hold down a job, or set the pace for family activities. However, their value is greater to their loved ones than ever before. Only age can bring about wisdom, and this wisdom must be passed down through the generations if we are to learn from our past.

I have a relative now in her eighties who spends a considerable amount of time writing letters to yet unborn grandchildren and great-grandchildren, passing on wisdom her life experiences have taught her. I have not read these letters, but I am confident they will be cornerstones for future generations. And as it is said in Proverbs 8:11, "For wisdom is far more valuable than rubies. Nothing you desire can compare with it." Only age and life experiences can bring the type of wisdom that may sustain the next generation.

"A love of books, of holding a book, turning its pages, looking at its pictures, and living it's fascinating stories goes hand-in-hand with a love of learning."

Laura Bush,
Former First Lady of the United States

# What's Up Doc?

"If we encounter a man of rare intellect, we should ask him what books he reads."

Ralph Waldo Emerson,
American Writer

My cousin Stephen has the distinction of being in possession of our family's only PhD. He has spent most of his life in college academia. After constant prodding from his very proud grandmother, Molly, he begrudgingly showed up at an occasional reunion of her ancestral clan. At these events, he patiently endured countless questions from relatives who assumed everyone who had "Dr." as a surname was from the medical profession. Of course, the bar was set pretty low with us as cosmetology, welding, and truck driving schools were considered "higher education."

When it came to testing Stephen's patience, Aunt Fred was the masterful ringleader. She always had an arsenal of rapid-fire questions as she sought free advice about the most effective home remedies for a litany of ailments such as her bunions or Uncle Fern's chronic bouts with gout. I will never forget the look on Fred's face when Stephen reached the saturation level of her incessant prodding. She asked if she should use caster or cod liver oil to stop her granddaughter from sucking her thumb. His response went right over her head when he said, "It depends on if you are baking or grilling her."

After fulfilling his obligation, Stephen would retreat to his home, which was a library unto itself. Every wall was lined with floor-to-ceiling bookshelves containing his expansive book collection. He was always very gracious to share any of his books with a family member, friend, or student needing guidance with a term paper.

Stephen and his wife, Shanna, also a professor, did not have children, and she died of cancer relatively young. After her passing, the reclusive Stephen withdrew even deeper into his books, intellectual discussions, and academic pursuits.

I always wondered what was going to happen to all those books after his death. The answer came in an unexpected package along with a letter I received recently.

The letter was from Stephen, and it was direct and to the point. He said age and other health issues were taking their toll, and it was impossible to maintain his two-story home. Therefore, he had chosen to spend his last years in a retirement center owned and managed by his beloved college. Before the move, he was taking special care to dismantle his collection of over one thousand books which had brought him so much joy and comfort over the years. With the advent of electronic books, book tablets, and audiobooks, his collection was less desirable to local libraries. Therefore, he was distributing as much of his collection as possible to friends, family, neighbors, colleagues, and former students.

He forwarded two books to me, and both came with a personal inscription. One book was titled *The Great Buffalo Hunt* by Wayne Gard, and it was originally inscribed to Stephen from my father. In writing his re-inscription to me, Stephen wrote, "I was so honored to receive this first edition classic book from your dad in 1967. We once visited about our mutual fascination with the old west, and he thought I would enjoy this book from his own library." The other book was William Manchester's *The Last Lion/Visions of Glory.* His inscription read, "This book about Winston Churchill is one of my all-time favorites. I know you have a great interest in ordinary people who become extraordinary leaders during challenging times, and I thought you would find this book exceptional." I am so honored Stephen chose me to keep these special message books in the family for another generation.

I know from my own experience of dismantling my parent's library, it can be a difficult, emotional task. Before turning most of their books over to a garage sale, I went through every one of them and found it impossible to discard any of the books that had personal inscriptions.

### Preserving the Written Word / Preserving Your History

Writing meaningful inscriptions in books is almost a lost art, but these written words are a great way to preserve family history and pass on words of wisdom to future generations.

I have another cousin who was inspired by Steven's gesture, and he is spending some of his retirement time going through his book collection and writing personal notes to grandchildren of why he wants them to have this specific book, why it had special meaning to him, and what he hoped the recipient would glean from it.

# Life in the Shadow of a Steeple— The Legacy of Fred and Fern

One hot Wednesday evening when I was a young boy, my grandparents coaxed me to join them in attending a Wednesday night prayer meeting in a neighboring town where Uncle Fern was the preacher. At these mid-week gatherings, Fern's message was slightly more subdued; however, he did manage to inject a fire and brimstone zinger here and there.

On the last Wednesday of every month after the prayer meeting, there was a much-anticipated pot-luck supper in the church fellowship hall. All participants brought their favorite covered dishes of green bean casseroles, macaroni and cheese, pound cake, or Jell-O fruit salad drowning in whip cream and pecans (when in season). Of course, the highlight of these events was always Aunt Fred's signature potato salad.

These simple gatherings offered a rare opportunity for these hard-working rural parishioners to socialize. Uncle Fern always maintained the pious dignity expected of the preacher, but occasionally his deep belly laugh echoed throughout the hall. Oddly enough, this was the only time anyone could ever remember seeing Aunt Fred "almost" smile. Hardly a smile, it was just a subtle upturn in her lips when receiving compliments about her potato salad. All requests for her carefully guarded recipe were politely shunned.

Fred and Fern lived contentedly as they tended their flocks in various small-town churches. Their movements are forever charted in letters written to family members from Aunt Fred announcing the change of address to a new "parish house" in a new community. If one looked closely at their journey, it was obvious that late in life, their moves were more frequent, and the church communities grew smaller with each move. But Fred always spoke positively about the adequacy of the new church-provided parish house, its convenience to the church, and the virtues of their new community.

Unfortunately, Fern's good fortunes took an unexpected turn late in his career when a very young parishioner turned up pregnant, and, to everyone's shock, she identified Fern as the father. As standard protocol, the national church organization had to investigate, and Fern was temporarily removed from the pulpit. While Fred was incensed, Fern took it in stride and even joked it could be another immaculate conception if a seventy-year-old man, dealing with his second bout of prostate cancer, could father a child.

During this time, Fred and Fern left town and moved in with their daughter and her family. Fern found meaningful work offering spiritual counseling and comfort to residents at a local nursing home. His attitude was, "God brought me here for a reason, and this is good enough for me." He also admitted that due to his declining health, it was probably a blessing to give up the pulpit—something he would never have done on his own.

The investigation totally exonerating Fern of any wrongdoing was completed only months before his death. As far as he was concerned, the case was closed. For Fred, it was another matter.

She started a major letter-writing campaign making sure everyone in the church knew of Fred's innocence. She also wanted the "tramp" who falsely accused Fern of wrongdoing to be kicked out of the church and driven out of town.

It was only after the love child was born and proved to be of mixed race, did Aunt Fred finally feel Fern was completely exonerated. She then changed her perspective and decided the accusatory girl, or hussy (as Fred called her), should be forced to stay in the town where she would have to "publicly accept her shame each and every day of her life."

Thus, is the legacy of Fred and Fern.

"I don't think about whether people will remember me or not. I've been an okay person. I've learned a lot. I've taught people a thing or two. That's what's important. Sooner or later the public will forget you, the memory of you will fade. What's important is the individuals you've influenced along the way."

Julia Child,
Legendary Author and Chef

# Treasures from Aunt Alma's Kitchen

My beloved Aunt Alma was an extraordinary cook. No family event was complete without Alma happily supervising all meals prepared with her unique sense of style and loving respect for family traditions. When unexpected guests showed up at her home, she could whip up a memorable, four-course gourmet meal in minutes with whatever she had available. She also loved making homemade biscuits over a campfire, and at the age of ninety-three, she started entering and winning chili cook-offs.

Most of all she loved providing meals to people in need. She was always the first to show up with an abundance of food to a home where there was a death, illness, or birth in the family. Often, she would cook all night to meet a family's needs. Sometimes she did not even know the family she was assisting. She just heard of the need and wanted to help.

One afternoon, I found Alma in her kitchen rummaging through drawers of recipes looking for a baked squash casserole recipe a niece had requested. I started perusing through these stacks of paper she had sprawled out across her kitchen table and realized these faded scraps held a unique part of our family history. Many recipes were attached to letters from ancestors, or they had special notes scrawled across them like: "I call this Uncle Hank's beef vegetable stew because he loves eating it when he comes in after a cold winter day on the tractor."

It did not take much encouragement from me to persuade Alma into putting her favorite family recipes in a book for family members. Some of my best quality time with her was assembling over seventy of her most cherished recipes and putting them in a cookbook titled: *Treasures from Alma's Kitchen.*

With an original printing of fifty copies of the book, she gave them to family members for Christmas. That was followed by an additional one hundred printings to give to friends, and then their friends wanted copies. Before Alma passed away at the age of ninety-five, she had signed and given away over four hundred copies of her book! She has been gone now for over a decade. However, her book is considered a family treasure. All our family members have a much-used copy in their own kitchens.

Scattered throughout the cookbook are photos of family members and stories about a remembrance of a specific recipe. Alma wrote the forward herself:

Dear Family and Friends,

When I was six years old, my father hoisted me up on a chair in front of our kitchen stove so that I could help make breakfast for my brothers and sisters. My mother had just given birth to her sixth and final child, and I wanted to pitch in to help our growing family. This experience began my love affair with cooking, and it is something that I have enjoyed all my life.

Recently, I celebrated my eighty-sixth birthday. And it dawned on me that this year I would also celebrate eighty years of cooking. In recognition of this milestone, I decided to gather some of my favorite recipes, photos, and cooking experiences together to share with friends and family who have meant so much to me over the years.

Many of these recipes are original creations that have evolved over the years. Some date back to my grandmother, who brought them to America from our native Germany. And some of them are special recipes given to me by other families.

Food stimulates the senses, and each recipe brings back heartwarming memories of places, times, and people that have enriched my life. Whether it was preparing childhood dishes under my mother's watchful eye, serving up gourmet breakfasts over an open campfire, an intimate dinner for my husband and me, or a buffet feast for fifty, I have loved it all.

For eighty years, sharing the treasures from my kitchen has always brought me the greatest joy. This book is meant to be another extension of that shared love. I hope you enjoy it.

And remember, Alma's kitchen is always open.

Love,
Alma

> ### Preserving the Written Word/ Preserving Your History
>
> Modern desktop technology has made compiling a family cookbook very easy. Moreover, these homemade books offer a creative way to preserve family recipes, bygone traditions, and old photos. They can be written in a manner where a simple cookbook becomes a cherished archive of family history that lasts for generations.

# That Darn Tangled Web Nabs Aunt Fred

One of Aunt Fred's favorite criticisms of me and the rest of humanity was a very annoying verse she said incessantly, "Oh, what a tangled web we weave when first we practice to deceive."

Therefore, I took great joy when a cousin recently found a recipe in Aunt Fred's belongings that betrayed a falsehood about her "famous" potato salad, which she perpetuated all her life. The salad was a heralded hit at all family and social gatherings. But Aunt Fred refused to ever share the recipe. She just said she mixed things together until it met her taste approval. However, it turns out the salad was the creation of one of our pioneer aunts who shared it with Fred in a letter dated 1958.

It is only right that Aunt Fred's lifelong potato salad malfeasance be exposed.

FYI—a cousin recently made this dish exactly as the

pioneer recipe instructed for a family reunion. By all accounts, it was truly amazing. We all agreed the homemade pickles, radishes, mustard seeds, and the lack of preservatives made this a truly unique and delicious salad. Attempt making it if you dare.

Prep time: six months

*Ingredients*

Red pepper powder (a.k.a. paprika)

Always keep a couple of red pepper plants around the house. (They need lots of sun but don't need special soil and very little water.) When the peppers start to fall off the stalk, place them in a sunny windowsill to completely dry out. Then use a rolling pin to crush the peppers as fine as you can get them. *The pepper can be stored in a jar for a year.*

Homemade pickles (a.k.a. dill pickles minus calcium chloride, sodium benzoate, alum., polysorbate 80, and yellow 5)

Sterilize 6 mason jars and pack with sliced medium or small cucumbers. Boil 4 cups of water, 1 cup vinegar, and 4 tablespoons of salt for about five minutes and pour into each jar. Add to each jar three sprigs of dill, one clove of garlic, and a tablespoon of honey. Seal the jars and process them by lowering each jar into a large pot of water. Bring water to a light boil for ten minutes. Store in your root cellar or kitchen cabinet for six weeks before eating.

Egg custard (a.k.a. mayonnaise minus high fructose corn syrup, modified cornstarch, added salt, and potassium sorbate)

Place 4 yolks from freshly laid eggs in a bowl and slowly add in 2 cups of cooking oil as you blend ingredients. Stir in 2 tablespoons of lemon juice. If you don't have lemons, you can use vinegar. (Apple cider vinegar works well.) Place in icebox overnight before using.

Dark mustard seed sauce (a.k.a. Dijon mustard minus 125 mg. of added salt)

Get the darkest mustard seeds you can find at your store. Use your coffee grinder to grind up ½ cup of seeds. Pour seeds in a bowl and add ½ cup of room temperature water. (Or if you want to be adventurous, use ½ cup of beer.) Add two tablespoons of honey and 4 tablespoons of finely chopped fresh parsley. This will store in the icebox for up to six months.

*Day of Assembly*

Peel and cook 6 Idaho potatoes (give them a rough mash)
Add 5 hardboiled eggs (chopped)
1 cup of finely chopped celery
½ cup diced onion
½ cup chopped pickles
1 tablespoon of mustard seed sauce (Dijon mustard)
2 tablespoons (or more) of egg custard (mayonnaise)
3 finely chopped radishes when in season
Mix well and top with a generous amount of pepper powder (paprika)
Cool in icebox for three to five hours before serving

'Tis the gift to be simple 'tis the gift to be free, 'tis the gift to come down where we ought to be, and when we find ourselves in the place just right. 'Twill be n the valley of love and delight. When true simplicity is gained.

*Simple Gifts* Shaker Hymn,
Aaron Copland

# The Art of Simplicity—Fred and Fern Buck a Trend

"This is all that I have learned: God made us plain and simple, but we have made ourselves very complicated" (Ecclesiastes 7:29, GNT).

Looking back at the lives of Aunt Fred and Uncle Fern, one would observe an almost arcane and peculiar existence. Yet, when compared to today's rat race, they may have just hit on something we can all benefit from.

One hot August afternoon of my youth, my mom and grandparents gave me an option. I could help empty-nesters Aunt Fred and Uncle Fern pack up to move or spend the day visiting relatives in surrounding nursing homes. Neither option sounded very appealing, but I took the moving option.

It was the right choice as moving Fred and Fern took less than thirty minutes. They each had a small tattered suitcase, both held together with duct tape, which contained their meager personal belongings. There was one box for books (mostly Bibles) and the photo album, a box for keepsake knick-knacks, old chipped dishes, along with a few bedroom and bathroom linens. Fern strung a clothes bar across the backseat of the car, which held his three suits, a few dress shirts, and a couple of ties. On Fred's side, there were four solid-colored dresses, a patched winter coat, and a sweater she knitted herself.

All parish houses were the same. The small non-descript functional structures attached to the church property were adorned with hand-me-down furnishings that some members of the congregation chose to donate to the church rather than make a trip out to the local dump. So, the need to move furniture was never an option.

All of Fred and Fern's belongings fit comfortably in their used Ford sedan with its ragged upholstery, a perpetually cracked windshield, and a non-existent muffler. They must have gone through several used cars during the time I remember them; however, the vehicles always looked the same. The last moving ritual was complete when Fred carefully placed three coffee cans containing her pride and joy red chili pepper vines on the backseat floorboard.

They dropped me off at my grandparent's farm, made me promise to be good, and hand-in-hand off they went on a new adventure to serve their beloved God and a new flock in need of saving. Aunt Fred's parting words were, "Tell everyone I will write as soon as we get our new address." I have to say, they seemed at peace with their simple, unencumbered lives as they drove away in a trail of backroad summer dust.

# A Shoebox Surprise

The last letter in my family's Shoebox history was, ironically, written by me over forty years ago. I had completely forgotten about it, but it was treasured for a lifetime by the recipient.

My college psychology professor gave us an assignment to write a letter to someone we cared about and to convey sentiments to them we had struggled to express. This exercise was modeled after an effective therapeutic protocol in drug and alcohol treatment centers.

I have no recollection of the letter I finally submitted for this project. One draft was to my father, and I never intended for him to read it. However, to my great surprise, I found the crumpled-up draft among his very small collection of saved personal items.

The fact he somehow found the draft, read it, and kept it his entire life gave me great peace of mind.

Dear Dad,

At the end of one normal school day, I climbed on the bus for my quick trip home. The bus was a little more crowded this afternoon. It seemed a bunch of girls from my fourth-grade class got on, all wearing Girl Scout uniforms. I would sneak a glance at them when I thought none of them were looking. I had not decided to talk to girls yet, and I wasn't going to start now. As I thought this over in my mind, I figured they were on their way to a Girl Scout meeting at Wilson's house down the street.

The bus made its usual stop at the top of the hill. The regular kids from the neighborhood got off along with me and the Girl Scouts. Even though our house was one of the first houses we came to, most days I slowed myself down getting home by climbing a tree or playing catch with some neighborhood kids. I would do anything to delay what was waiting for me at home: homework.

But on this day, I ran past everyone and arrived in our yard ahead of the pack. As I waited for the Girl Scouts to catch up, I slowly walked around and across our yard before entering our home, clearly in plain sight for everyone to see.

Our home on the corner lot stood out from the others. We had beautiful trees and a perfectly manicured lawn. I was proud for all my classmates to see where I lived. Your hard work and dedication to our family provided that moment for me. Looking back, I realized I took part in it, too. My Saturday mornings were spent mowing the lawn to your specifications, raking leaves, and setting the water sprinklers per your instructions. I know I complained about doing the chores at the time, but at that moment, it became clear to me the lesson you wanted me to learn: hard work created the beautiful yard I was so proud of.

Your devotion to our family did not go unnoticed, although I rarely acknowledged it to you. That is the reason for this letter. I am proud to be your son, and you made us a proud family.

Love,
Mark

# Will the Circle Be Unbroken?

I have been amazed by the response *The Shoebox Chronicles* has received since I found that old box of letters under my parent's bed several years ago. Regularly, I hear stories of family members who have been inspired to leave their own legacy by connecting the dots of their past.

That point was emphasized recently when I received an invitation to a family reunion from Aunt Fred's granddaughter, Francis. The social media invite read: "Bring your family, old letters, diaries, photos, recipes, and Bibles as we celebrate with an old-fashioned family reunion."

By all estimates, this was our first family reunion since my grandmother's generation, and I was very humbled the event was dubbed "The Shoebox Reunion." I decided to go even though I would know almost no one in attendance.

The event was held on a wonderful spring day at an open-air pavilion on the banks of the Brazos River in central Texas. When I arrived, most of the people were enjoying the outdoors playing games, sampling an assortment of old family recipes, or engaged in conversation as relatives connected the dots of their lives. My first observance when entering the yard was how wonderfully diverse our family had become, with almost all ethnicities represented. Several men were proudly wearing Jewish skull caps (yarmulkes) while a mother and daughter team donned the traditional Muslim headscarf.

I mingled through the crowd and found my cousin Francis who was busy coordinating the upcoming "Aunt Fred Potato Salad Contest." After exchanging pleasantries and other introductions, I remarked how the contest would have made Aunt Fred so happy. Francis looked puzzled by my comment, and I was stunned by her response; "You know she's here. Would you like to meet her?" Had I known Aunt Fred was still alive, I would have probably treated her with a little more deference when writing the Chronicles.

Francis escorted me over to a wheelchair-bound woman sitting contently under a shade tree, just soaking in the activities. As we approached her, my cousin explained she was one hundred two years old with a relatively sharp mind but suffered from the onset of Parkinson's. I had not seen her in fifty years, but I recognized her immediately.

Fortunately, my tensions about my writings were eased when she told me how much she loved the blog and how she looked forward to every time her niece came to the nursing home with a laptop in tow to read the latest edition. As she dozed in and out of conversations, we pretty much exhausted all topics related to family and our shared past.

I then, hesitantly, brought up the question I wanted to ask all day, "Aunt Fred, looking back over your life, do you have any regrets?" She immediately answered she regretted ever letting herself be stuck with that "god-awful" nickname. But then she pondered the question for a long time, took a deep breath, and said, "Of course, I was very narrow-minded back in my day. But I can't apologize for that. I really didn't know any better. My grandmother and mother both married ministers so it was only natural I followed suit. We felt it was our moral obligation to support our husbands' ministries by upholding the highest standards of the church. At the time, those church views were pretty puritan."

With sadness, she did recount the biggest regret of her life. It was just too much for her to accept when her only son, Frank, announced he was marrying a Roman Catholic and converting to Catholicism. She didn't speak to him for three years. Finally, one day she just drove over to his home with his favorite casserole in hand. He acted as if the separation had never happened. With tears in her eyes, she recounted, "Frank died at the age of sixty-four from that horrible prostate cancer that plagues so many of you men in the family. To this day, I regret those years of his life I missed."

After a long pause to compose herself, she said, "But I learned something from it. The pretty girl in blue coming this way is Frank's youngest daughter Fredricka. Despite my warnings, she goes by Fred. Last month I attended her wedding as she married the love of her life, a sweet nurse named Jennifer. Whether it is right or wrong is between her and her God, and I'm not going to judge. But I do know I love my granddaughter with all my heart, and I am not going to let one minute of discourse come between us in the twilight of my life."

Her parting comment brought us full circle: "Fredricka is just like the rest of Fern's side of the family. Looking at our family history shows you guys have always tested the limits of the accepted norms of your times, and all these people here today have learned from it and are better for it. Knowing their family history is everything."

As the day drew to a close and people prepared to depart with the promise to write real letters, we resumed a family tradition from decades earlier. From old letters between my grandmother (Gram) and her sisters, we learned all family reunions ended with everyone joining hands and singing *Will the Circle be Unbroken.* As I stepped away from the circle, I could not help but think of Gram and her sisters and how happy this gathering would have made them. Their saved letters brought us together, and I am confident a renewed interest in meaningful written communications will inspire future generations to document and preserve their family history.

# Epilogue

It is hard to believe it has been over three years since I first discovered that dusty old shoebox of letters while dismantling my parents' homestead. What started as a tribute to my family and their dedication to the written word has blossomed into a devoted group of followers of my blog *The Shoebox Chronicles.* People have been awakened to realize the importance of preserving their own family history. What I gleaned from the original letters is that we are all making our own history, and it is our responsibility to share our stories with future generations. Only through our written and saved words can these histories be accurately documented in family archives.

The first question people ask when reading these stories is, "Are they true?" The answer is yes and sort of. Some of the reproduced letters are printed as written. However, I do admit to using a writer's creative license when telling some of these stories. I also had to make some assumptions about long-departed relatives when their complete story could not be validated. However, all stories are based on real people and known facts about their lives, and I am confident I connected the dots of our family history through six generations with fidelity.

I want to extend a sincere thank you to all my family members and close family friends, many of whom I have only recently met. A heartfelt thank you for sharing your family letters, diaries, and stories with me. I did my best to do your family justice in this book.

I also want to especially thank my de facto "Editor-in-Chief," John Harrell, for keeping me on track with my storylines while spending countless hours correcting my spelling, punctuation, and unique approach to sentence structure. He once lamented he had gone through an entire box of red pens to get these stories ready for publication. As he said often, there was a reason I chose Accounting, not English, as a college major. A darn good reason!

Finally, thank you to my loyal, devoted blog readers for your encouragement to complete this project and submit it for public review.

# About the Author

In December 2019, Mark Lehman retired from a long, successful career in public policy to pursue volunteer activities, writing, and public speaking. Lehman has authored several scripts for movies and television, in addition to his blog, *The Shoebox Chronicles,* which includes a global following of thousands of readers. Most of his volunteer efforts are focused on the medical, spiritual, and provisional needs of Austin's homeless community, in addition to his work as a Riverbend Church Foundation Board Member.

We make plans, but God makes detours to those plans. On the first day of quarantine due to the pandemic, Lehman was diagnosed with Stage 3 melanoma. This resulted in major surgery, followed by ongoing treatment at the renowned MD Anderson Cancer Center in Houston, Texas. Mark faced cancer with a brave spirit, and he believes it was a blessing rather than a curse. The quarantine, along with his medical issues, has allowed him to laser-focus his life on what's important: doing God's will for the greater good. Facing the demon of cancer head-on, Mark has entrenched himself in philanthropic endeavors to erase cancer for good.

Mark splits his time between his beloved hometown of Austin, Texas, and Red Lodge, Montana.

The author takes no profits from the sale of this book. All profits are donated to charity.

# Endnotes

[1] Zionist: People dedicated to the formation and protection of a Jewish nation in what is now Israel.